Comprehensive Homeschool Records

Put Your Best Foot Forward to Win College Admission and Scholarships

Lee Binz,
The HomeScholar

First Printing, 2015

Printed in the United States of America

ISBN: 151141703X
ISBN-13: 978-1511417037

Disclaimer: Parents assume full responsibility for the education of their children in accordance with state law. College requirements vary, so make sure to check with the colleges about specific requirements for homeschoolers. We offer no guarantees, written or implied, that the use of our products and services will result in college admissions or scholarship awards.

Comprehensive Homeschool Records

Put Your Best Foot Forward
to Win College Admission
and Scholarships

What are
"Coffee Break Books"?

"Comprehensive Homeschool Records" is part of The HomeScholar's Coffee Break Book series.

Designed especially for parents who don't want to spend hours and hours reading a 400-page book on homeschooling high school, each book combines Lee's practical and friendly approach with detailed, but easy-to-digest information, perfect to read over a cup of coffee at your favorite coffee shop!

Never overwhelming, always accessible and manageable, each book in the series will give parents the tools they need to tackle the tasks of homeschooling high school, one warm sip at a time.

Everything about these Coffee Break Books is designed to suggest simplicity, ease and comfort - from the size (fits in a purse), to the font and paragraph length (easy on the eyes), to the price (the same as a Starbucks Venti Triple Caramel Macchiato). Unlike a fancy coffee drink, however, these books are guilt-free pleasures you will want to enjoy again and again!

Table of Contents

Preface

Why This Book?

The purpose of this little book is to share with you the single most important strategy our family used to secure a full tuition scholarship for each of our two boys. These were two of ten scholarships available, given the same year, given by the same college, to two children in the same family. One boy was 18 and the other 16. Both boys were homeschooled independently through high school. Neither received any outside coaching or tutoring. It was just their dad and me, the dog and a whole lot of books. We didn't have enough money saved for college. In fact, I was going to have to go back to work full time in order to even begin to afford college. We were looking at a mountain of bills and my kids were looking at a mountain of debt.

Yet, despite the odds, we got scholarships from our first choice university, worth over $187,000.

Sure, we were serious about our academics, but we only did school four days a week, so I suppose we weren't THAT serious. Plus, we committed what might be considered a mortal sin for students seeking scholarships... we had almost zero volunteer hours (shocking, I know).

My husband and I aren't rocket scientists. We are both products of a "normal public school education." We certainly aren't rich and we, like many of you, homeschooled on a very tight budget.

All this to say: we were really nothing special. Even our desperation wasn't that special as it is shared by every parent staring down the barrel of $50,000 - $60,000 in annual tuition bills for four consecutive years.

But we were resourceful and, dare I say, a bit creative. We developed a strategy that was, at the time, almost unheard of by college admissions officials. We didn't know if it would work, but it was the only page in our songbook so we sang it with gusto.

Now, I want to share that strategy with you - both what it is and why it worked so brilliantly. Our prayer is that you will see how a bit of grit and determination can change the course of history for an entire family. Although this is not a detailed guidebook - there are other resources I will share with you - I know the most resourceful of you will find all the samples you need here to build your own homeschool records from scratch. Our goal is much more modest. We want to inspire you to finish your homeschooling journey and when it is time, to give the colleges your very best shot. Who knows, you may live to someday tell your own miraculous tale!

Introduction

Disco (and Affordable College) is Dead

I used to hate when my parents said, "back in my day…" Now that I'm the parent, I find myself thinking (if not outright saying) the same thing. One of my frequent laments is "Back in my day, going to college wasn't so complex."

Maybe you remember when…

- College was almost affordable
- Almost everyone who wanted to go, got to go
- Most kids graduated with little or no debt
- College scholarships weren't so incredibly competitive.

Those days are as dated as my husband's dance moves (sorry, honey...) College admissions is a high stakes business now and homeschool parents often feel ill-equipped to compete with public and private schools in gaining admission and scholarships.

In fact, the competitive nature of the college admissions game has bred an entire industry of private, college prep schools characterized by advanced placement academics, college admission coaches, elite sports leagues, "drill and kill" test prep and enough volunteer work to inspire Mother Teresa.

It is almost a David and Goliath story. In this corner stands the thoroughly modern two income family with their SAT coaches, college consultants and elite academics. In the opposite corner stands the typical homeschool family with their limited financial resources, do-it-yourself guidance counseling and home-grown academics.

So whose kids do you think have the edge in the college admission and scholarship sweepstakes: the normal homeschooled college-ready kid or the super-charged private and public school kid? Well, the answer may surprise you.

Chapter 1

What Are Colleges Looking For, Really?

If you were to answer this question just based on the goings-on in a typical college prep high school you would probably conclude that colleges were only interested in three types of students:

- AP Wizards. After all, why go to all that trouble trying to pass so many of those insanely difficult exams?
- Athletic Powerhouses. Nothing else could explain the intensity of today's most competitive high school sports teams.
- Academic Elites. Why else would parents spend thousands to get

their kids those fabled "perfect SAT scores?"

So if your homeschool doesn't have a laser focus on these "three As", how can you possibly hope to compete?

Oh, and if you aren't relentless in your pursuit of extra-curriculars, and working diligently on padding your child's resume with volunteer and community activities (sometimes at the expense of family harmony and parental sanity), how can you even dream of getting a place at the table? The answer is simple, really...

It's because this ISN'T what the colleges are looking for.

So, What Are Colleges REALLY Looking For?

In my business, I have spent a lot of time researching and speaking to colleges. My conclusion is that colleges have three and ONLY three questions about every prospective candidate:

- Are they REAL?
- Are they READY?
- Are they RIGHT?

1. Are They REAL?

Whether it is in the realm of academics, athletics or activities, colleges are most concerned about whether an applicant is authentic. Is that burning passion they see because their soul is on fire, or because dad lit their pants on fire? If there's one thing a college admissions official can root out faster than a ghost-written admission essay, it's a phony high school senior.

2. Are They READY?

In simple terms, that means making sure your kids cover the basics well; reading, writing, math. It also means getting your kids around people of all different ages and socio-economic statuses. With all the grief homeschool parents receive about "socialization" it is a bit ironic that the key to college academic and emotional readiness turns out to be the type of socialization that homeschoolers are best capable to deliver: the type of socialization that comes from being "out and about" in the real world, rather than stuck in a classroom.

3. Are They RIGHT?

Not every university will fit every student. More importantly, not every student will fit every university. Colleges want to know whether your student's ideals, values and perspective are a good match for them. Heck, just the fact that your student has ideals, values and perspective will be appealing simply because it brings a bit of diversity compared to what colleges normally deal with!

Why is This So Important?

Colleges are BIG business. Like any business, they seek to enhance their reputation and extend their influence. One of the primary paths to do this is through admission of highly qualified students. Students who promise to distinguish themselves in the world of politics, business, science, sports or the arts.

There are two primary reasons it is important for colleges to have industry and political leaders shine their light back and give them credit for launching their careers. The first is obvious. It can never hurt to have a community of wealthy benefactors to provide ongoing endowments and scholarships. The other is a bit more subtle, but has to do with the perpetuation of their brand and image.

Here is an illustration. Everyone knows that Barak Obama graduated from Harvard Law, but who do you think has benefitted most from that fact – President Obama or Harvard Law? Do you see the symbiotic relationship between colleges and their prospective students? Just like you have a vested interest in gaining admission and scholarships, they have a vested interest in finding the best.

Chapter 2

Watch Out For This Trap!

Just understanding what the colleges value isn't enough. So, what action needs to be taken? Homeschool parents (and especially homeschool dads) may grow frantic about making their kids "Real, Ready, and Right" for college. In their fervor, they might attempt to out "prep" the prep schools.

Don't do this. It is a trap.

The worst thing you can do is try to play their game. That just leads to frenzy, frustration, and failure. Instead, a better approach is to perform a bit of educational judo and turn the "weaknesses" of homeschooling (as perceived by the world), into strengths.

An Unleveled Playing Field

One of the greatest advantages that homeschoolers have over kids from most public and private high schools is the opportunity to enjoy life-defining experiences during the normal course of the school year. As I mentioned, we purposefully homeschooled only 4 days a week so our boys had time to get "out there" and discover their passion in the adult world.

That passion will bear fruit when preparedness meets opportunity. Done properly, homeschooling is the best life preparation available. But opportunity...

That's the problem.

The ugly truth is that opportunity can be pretty hard for a public school kid to discover when they're strapped to a school desk for 6 hours a day, spend two hours a day on the bus, five more doing homework and then eight sleeping.

That's 21 hours of prescheduled time, 5 days a week. When you are trying to squeeze the rest of life into the remaining 3 hours, some things are bound to be missed; little things like purpose, passion and opportunity.

The Critical Difference

The way your kids will compete -- and compete successfully -- is by simply being different. That's right...it is OK to be different from the cookie cutter kids being produced by the typical public high school or even the typical college prep school.

In fact, it is CRITICAL to be different. And who, more than homeschoolers, are better equipped to produce "different" children? Let's be honest with ourselves, homeschool kids ARE different, primarily because they are differently nurtured, differently educated and differently socialized. This is a GOOD THING!

Don't fall into the trap of trying to replicate public and private high schools. Don't worry about passing 6 AP exams, or excelling in a different select sport every season, or getting a top dollar scholarship coach. Instead (and this is critical)...

Focus on helping your student become the person God created them to be.

That's right. It's that simple. Raising your children to be true to how they were made is the quickest and easiest path to college admission and scholarships. You don't have to change your homeschool to mimic the public and private schools – you can do what works. You don't have to choose curriculum you SHOULD use – you can use what works.

Now take a deep breath in....and out....and relax.

The delightful truth is that what colleges really want, is what you are already best qualified to deliver: confident, mature teens who know themselves and have had a LOT of time to pursue their passions!

OK, Now Prove It!

This becomes the key challenge of homeschooling high school with an eye toward college. How can you as parents document your homeschool so that colleges can quickly and accurately identify your student as the real deal? How do you demonstrate the authenticity and passion of your student rather than the teenage equivalent of vanilla pudding?

Is the answer spending your limited resources on accreditation agencies, getting the blessing of a certified teacher, or taking multiple AP exams?

No! The best strategy is often the simplest. The one that is easy. The one that feels right -- in a nutshell, the one that doesn't drive you or your children crazy. Your homeschooling high school should be done in a way that maximizes free time so the student can pursue their passion (while covering the basics). It should allow your student plenty of practice in the adult world to socialize with EVERYONE.

In simple terms this means:

- Students: Your responsibility is to prepare yourself academically and develop your career interests.
- Parents: In addition to helping your student prepare for college, your greatest responsibility is to follow along behind them and sweep up all those great experiences into believable and professional looking high school records.

One of the most effective tools for this is the comprehensive record.

Chapter 3

Comprehensive Record Crash Course

An effective comprehensive record will present your student as multi-dimensional, authentic, experienced, confident and ready for prime time! In addition to reflecting core education (the oft-overlooked three Rs of reading, writing and arithmetic), the comprehensive record will explicitly address the three Rs of any college-bound high schooler –- Are they Real? Are they Ready? Are they Right?

The finished product will be an authoritative record of your student's education. So authoritative and compelling, in fact, that colleges may tell you they have never seen anything like it before!

Of course, that can be good or bad, depending on how you prepare and present the information.

What Does a Comprehensive Record Look Like?

It's really not fair to tell you why comprehensive records are so important and then not show you what one looks like. This is a small book, so I can't paste in an entire comprehensive record, but I can describe it for you and give some examples.

Creating a comprehensive record is very much like cooking Thanksgiving dinner. There are unlimited options of the kinds of pies that you could make. There are many right ways to serve your pie, even if your mother-in-law says one thing, you can still do it in the right way in a different way, and you get to choose what works for your family.

You do need an ingredient list. A comprehensive record can include any or all of the following:

- Table of Contents – so they know what's inside at a glance
- Transcript – required by most, if not all, colleges
- Course Descriptions – titles, list of what you used, what you did, and a description of how you determined the grade you gave them
- Reading List
- Activities and Awards List
- Work Samples

When viewed as a whole, these elements might seem pretty overwhelming. However, each of them separately is not that difficult to create. For example, any of you who have purchased my Total Transcript Solution know that making a transcript can be pretty easy and (dare I say) even a little fun! The other elements of the comprehensive record are also relatively easy to break into component pieces and complete.

Table of Contents

The table of contents is kind of like the menu you get at a restaurant. It's going to be what shows the college admission representative exactly what your comprehensive record includes. You want to have that one-page "Transcript" listed at the top of your table of contents, and behind the table of contents will be your "Course Descriptions with Texts Used and Grading Criteria". Label each course underneath carefully, e.g. "English 1: American Literature and Composition". You will want to continue with a "Reading List", "Activities and Awards List" (both of which you may want to break down by year), and "Work Samples". And don't forget the page numbers for each item listed on your table of contents!

Providing page numbers can help because sometimes colleges don't want your records stapled in anyway, and those page numbers will help them find what they need. You can even use templates included in software such as Microsoft Word to create the table of contents to make it nice and easy.

Transcripts

In terms of your meal, the transcript is kind of like the appetizer; it's designed to whet the appetite of the college admission representative. It's the first page they see and it's an overview that's going to help them give a quick "thumbs up" or a "thumbs down" on the student. It's usually required by colleges, so be sure to include it. You can add course details as appropriate, knowing that the transcript is truly the backbone of the comprehensive record.

Since transcripts are the core of the comprehensive record, here are two example transcripts we prepared for our own children. This has been, by far, (whether you organize it by subject or by year), the most popular and most successful transcript format we have come across.

Transcript by Subject:

> ## OFFICIAL TRANSCRIPT
> ### ~Homeschool Senior High~

Homeschool Senior High
*Street Address * My City, WA 98123*

Student: Last, First   **Gender**: Male
Birth Date: 09/09/99
Parents: M/M Lastname   **Address:** Street Address, My City, WA 98123

Academic Record by Subject

Course	Class Title	Completion Date	Credits	Grade
English	English 1: American Literature & Composition	06/03	1.0	4.0
	Novel Writing	06/04	1.0	4.0
	English 2: World Literature & Composition	06/04	1.0	4.0
	**English 3: Honors Literature & Composition	06/05	1.0	4.0
Math	Algebra 1	06/01	1.0	4.0
	Geometry	06/02	1.0	4.0
	Algebra 2	06/03	1.0	4.0
	Pre-Calculus	06/04	1.0	4.0
	Calculus	06/05	1.0	4.0
Science	Biology with Lab	06/03	1.0	4.0
	Chemistry with Lab	06/04	1.0	4.0
	Physics with Lab	06/05	1.0	4.0
Social Studies	**American History	06/03	1.0	4.0
	**Ancient World History	06/04	1.0	4.0
	Washington State History	06/04	0.5	4.0
	**Modern World History	06/05	1.0	4.0
	**American Government	06/05	1.0	4.0

Foreign Language	Latin 1	06/01	1.0	4.0
	Latin 2	06/02	1.0	4.0
	Latin 3	06/03	1.0	4.0
	French 1	11/02	1.0	4.0
	French 2	05/03	1.0	4.0
	French 3	06/04	1.0	4.0
Fine Arts	Music: Piano 2 with Performance	06/03	1.0	4.0
	Music: Piano 3 with Performance	06/04	1.0	4.0
	Music: Piano 4 with Performance	06/05	1.0	4.0
	Fine Arts 1: American Art	06/03	0.5	4.0
	Fine Arts 2: History of Art	06/04	0.5	4.0
	Fine Arts 3: Art and Music Appreciation	06/05	0.5	4.0
Bible	Bible: Christian Manhood	06/03	0.5	4.0
	Bible: Apologetics	06/04	0.5	4.0
	Bible: World View	06/05	0.5	4.0
Elective	Critical Thinking Chess	06/03	1.0	4.0
	Public Speaking	06/03	1.0	4.0
	Occupational Education	06/04	0.5	4.0
	Driver's Education	07/04	0.5	Pass
	Russian History	06/04	0.5	4.0
	Formal Logic	06/04	0.5	4.0
PE	PE 1	06/03	1.0	4.0
	PE 2	06/04	1.0	4.0
	PE 3	06/05	1.0	4.0
Activities:	Soccer Team 9, 10,11: Swim Team 9,10, 11 Coaches Award 10: Competitive Chess 9, 10, 11 Student Teacher 9,10, 11: Youth Mission Team 10: Youth Group 9, 10, 11: Worship 9,11			

SAT Results	Grade Point Equivalents	Summary	
March 2005: Reading 740, Math 710, Writing 760, Total 2210	A =90-100% =4.0	**Credits**	**GPA**
June 2005: Reading 790, Math 770, Writing 690, Total 2250	B=80-89% = 3.0	35.5	4.0
**Denotes Honors course, documented by passing CLEP exam	C=70-79% = 2.0		
	D = 60-69% = 1.0		

Transcript by Year:

OFFICIAL TRANSCRIPT
~Homeschool Senior High~

Homeschool Senior High
*1234 Street Dr. SW * City, WA 98166*

Student: Last, First　　**Gender**: Male
Birth Date: 09/09/99
Parents: M/M Lastname　　**Address:** Street Address, My City, WA 98123

Academic Record by Year

Year	Class Title	Completion Date	Credits	Grade
Early High School	Algebra 1	06/01	1.0	4.0
Credits	Latin 1	06/01	1.0	4.0
	Geometry	06/02	1.0	4.0
	Latin 2	06/02	1.0	4.0
	French 1	11/02	1.0	4.0
2002-2003	English 1: American Literature & Composition	06/03	1.0	4.0
	Algebra 2	06/03	1.0	4.0
	Biology with Lab	06/03	1.0	4.0
	**American History	06/03	1.0	4.0
	Latin 3	06/03	1.0	4.0
	French 2	05/03	1.0	4.0
	Music: Piano 2 with Performance	06/03	1.0	4.0
	Fine Arts 1: American Art	06/03	0.5	4.0
	Bible: Christian Manhood	06/03	0.5	4.0
	Critical Thinking Chess	06/03	1.0	4.0
	Public Speaking	06/03	1.0	4.0
	PE 1	06/03	1.0	4.0

2003-2004	English 2: World Literature & Composition	06/04	1.0	4.0
	Novel Writing	06/04	1.0	4.0
	Pre-Calculus	06/04	1.0	4.0
	Chemistry with Lab	06/04	1.0	4.0
	**Ancient World History	06/04	1.0	4.0
	Washington State History	06/04	0.5	4.0
	French 3	06/04	1.0	4.0
	Music: Piano 3 with Performance	06/04	1.0	4.0
	Fine Arts 2: History of Art	06/04	0.5	4.0
	Bible: Apologetics	06/04	0.5	4.0
	Occupational Education	06/04	0.5	4.0
	Russian History	06/04	0.5	4.0
	Formal Logic	06/04	0.5	4.0
	PE 2	06/04	1.0	4.0
	Driver's Education	07/04	0.5	4.0
2004-2005	**English 3: Honors Literature & Composition	06/05	1.0	4.0
	Calculus	06/05	1.0	4.0
	Physics with Lab	06/05	1.0	4.0
	**Modern World History	06/05	1.0	4.0
	**American Government	06/05	1.0	4.0
	Music: Piano 4 with Performance	06/05	1.0	4.0
	Fine Arts 3: Art and Music Appreciation	06/05	0.5	4.0
	Bible: World View	06/05	0.5	4.0
	PE 3	06/05	1.0	4.0

Activities:	Soccer Team 9, 10,11: Swim Team 9,10, 11 Coaches Award 10: Competitive Chess 9, 10, 11 Student Teacher 9,10, 11: Youth Mission Team 10: Youth Group 9, 10, 11: Worship 9, 11		
SAT Results March 2005: Reading 740, Math 710, Writing 760, Total 2210 June 2005: Reading 790, Math 770, Writing 690, Total 2250	Grade Point Equivalents A =90- 100% =4.0 B=80-89% = 3.0 C=70-79% = 2.0 D = 60- 69% = 1.0	**Summary** Credits GPA	
Graduation Date: Month and Year		35.5 4.0	

Course Descriptions

The next section is the meat and potatoes of a comprehensive record –the course descriptions. Course descriptions describe what you did, what you used, and how you graded. "What you did" is just a one paragraph, descriptive essay of your class. Think about it as a 5th grade writing assignment.

Include materials you used, such as your primary texts, supplements that you added, additional books for fun, field trips, and other activities. The list of items you graded on is not necessarily related to whether or not you gave tests.

In my homeschool, we only used tests for half of my homeschool classes, and we evaluated using things such as discussion, reports, and essays for the other classes.

Here is a course description from our own comprehensive record to give you an idea of the final product:

Sample Course Description
Social Studies: American History

This course is a literature-based study of American history, culture, and geography. A wide selection of biographies, American literature, art, music, historical fiction and poetry provide an in-depth understanding of the primary text. The student will discuss the impact that history has on current events. Reading is accompanied by oral reports and class discussion. Daily work includes primary source reading, narration, mapping activities, timeline activities, current events study, and worldview evaluation. Honors credit will be awarded upon successful completion of CLEP exam with passing score of 50 or greater. Written work available on request.

Primary Text:
The History of US series by Joy Hakim
The First Americans by Joy Hakim
Making Thirteen Colonies by Joy Hakim
From Colonies to Country by Joy Hakim
The New Nation by Joy Hakim
Liberty for All? by Joy Hakim
War, Terrible War, by Joy Hakim
Reconstruction and Reform, by Joy Hakim
An Age of Extremes by Joy Hakim
War, Peace, and All That Jazz by Joy Hakim
All the People by Joy Hakim
"Our Sacred Honor" Audiotape series by William J. Bennett
Sonlight Curriculum American History in Depth: Curriculum Guide

Supplemental Texts: See reading list

Current Events: Daily newspaper reading
Weekly "World Magazine" reading
WorldView Academy "WorldView & Apologetics
Lecture Series" audiotapes

Reports: The student will complete written reports throughout the course. The following reports are available on request: The Emancipation Proclamation, Dialog Interview with a Slave, The War in Iraq, The Vietnam War, Fidel Castro.

Course Grade
American History – Completed 06/03

Reading ----1/3 grade----		Daily Work ----1/3 grade------		Reports ------1/3 grade----
Semester 1	100%	Semester 1	100%	Emancipation Proclamation 100% Dialog: Interview a Slave 100%
Semester 2	100%	Semester 2	100%	War in Iraq 100% Fidel Castro 100% Vietnam War 100%
Final Grade	100%	Final Grade	100%	Final Grade 100%
----Final grade for American History = 100% = A ----				

CLEP Exam Score = 64 (ACE passing score 50)				
A =90-100% =4.0		B=80-89% = 3.0 D = 60-69% = 1.0		C=70-79% = 2.0

Reading List

The next thing you want to include is the reading list. It is kind of like getting to know someone over a coffee or tea, when you'll sort of sit back and sip your tea and get to know them through casual conversation. It's just a list; it's not a reading bibliography, so you don't have to include publishers, edition dates, or how many pages -- simply the title and the author. You may want to alphabetize the list to prevent duplicates.

You might have six or six hundred books -- each child is so unique. As long as your child has actually read some books and you've included some books that they've read, then it is fine to include audio books, books to movies, or plays. Just list them, for example, "War and Peace audio book". You can include reading that they did for school, reading for work, reading for pleasure, and goofy reading as well. I included twenty books on chess, which was the strange reading that my child loved.

Here is a page from my child's reading list. Every child is different. I had two prolific readers so this was probably larger than most reading lists:

20xx-20xy Reading List for Student Name

A Nation Challenged: A Visual History of 9/11 and its Aftermath by The New York Times
A Separate Peace by John Knowles
Alas, Babylon by Pat Frank
All Quiet on the Western Front by Erich Marla Remarque
Alpha for Youth by David C. Cook
Animal Farm by George Orwell
Autobiography of an Ex-Colored Man by James Weldon Johnson
Autobiography of Benjamin Franklin by Benjamin Franklin
Boy Meets Girl by Josh Harris
Brave New World by Aldous Huxley
Common Sense by Thomas Paine
Death Be Not Proud by John Gunther
Death of a Salesman by Arthur Miller
Dr. Jekyll and Mr. Hyde by Robert Louis Stevenson
Eats, Shoots, and Leaves by Lynne Truss
Elements of Style by Strunk and White
Flu: The Story of the Great Influenza Pandemic of 1918 by Gina Kolata
Frankenstein by Mary Shelley
Grapes of Wrath by John Steinbeck
Hard Times by Charles Dickens
Heart of Darkness by Joseph Conrad
Hiroshima by John Hershey
How to Write Poetry by Paul B. Janeczko
Icons of Evolution by Jonathan Wells
Invitation to the Classics by Louise Cowan and Os Guinness
Last of the Mohicans by James Fenimore Cooper
Life and Times of Frederick Douglass by Frederick Douglass
Life Lessons with Max Lucado: Book of Romans by Max Lucado
Literature: A Crash Course by Cory Bell
Literature: The American Experience by Prentice Hall
Lord of the Flies by William Golding
Murder at the Vicarage by Agatha Christie

Of Mice and Men by John Steinbeck

Oliver Twist by Charles Dickens

On Plymouth Rock by Samuel Drake

On the Duty of Civil Disobedience by Henry David Thoreau

Our Century in Pictures For Young People edited by Richard B. Stolley

Our Town by Thornton Wilder

Pickwick Papers by Charles Dickens

Poetry Speaks edited by Elise Paschen, Rebekah Mosby, et al.

Poor Richard's Almanac by Benjamin Franklin

Pride and Prejudice by Jane Austin

The Chosen by Chaim Potok

The Crucible by Arthur Miller

The Deadliest Monster by J. F. Baldwin

The Deerslayer by James Fenimore Cooper

The Great Gatsby by F. Scott Fitzgerald

The Jungle by Upton Sinclair

The Life and Times of Frederick Douglass by Frederick Douglass

The Little Regiment and other Civil War Stories by Stephen Crane

The Metamorphosis by Franz Kafka

The New Tolerance by Josh McDowell and Bob Hostetler

The Old Man and the Sea by Ernest Hemingway

The Pearl by John Steinbeck

The Privileged Planet by Guillermo Gonzalez and Jay Richards

The Right of Man by Thomas Paine

The Secret Sharer by Joseph Conrad

Up From Slavery by Booker T. Washington

Walden: or Life in the Woods by Henry David Thoreau

War of the Worlds by H.G. Wells

We Interrupt This Broadcast by Joe Garner

What We Saw: The Events of September 11, 2001 – in Words, Pictures and Video by CBS News

Audiotape:

Change and Motion: Calculus Made Clear by The Teaching Company

Einstein's Relativity and the Quantum Revolution The Teaching Company

European and Western Civilization in the Modern Age The Teaching Company

How to Listen to and Understand Great Music The Teaching Company

From Monet to Van Gogh: A History of Impressionism The Teaching Company

How to Read and Understand Poetry The Teaching Company
Economics The Teaching Company

Activities and Awards List

The next section to include in your comprehensive record is the activities and awards, which is kind of like the after dinner mint. This section will be a list of organizations or groups that your child was involved with, and any awards that they received, or positions they held in the group. If you had a lot of hours for activities, then you may want to make that a course. If you have 75 or more hours for a particular activity and it's something that's academic, you may want to list that for high school credit as a half-credit class, and also list it as an activity. If you have 90 to 120 hours for an activity, you may want to list that as a full-credit class, as well as an activity.

When I was in high school, I was very involved in high school choir. Every year, my transcript included 'Choir' with a grade beside it. When they asked us what activities we were involved with to put on my transcript, I also listed choir as an activity. It was put on my activity list and it was also a high school credit class. Your friends back in high school may have been involved in journalism or yearbook; those are also things that you might have listed as both an activity and a high school credit

Work Samples

Colleges may want to see work samples. These are like desserts –sweet tidbits of information about your child. Work samples might include samples of their writing and work samples from each course. This means that you do have to keep some records. One homeschool mom I know of had a bonfire party at the end of each year and burned all of their homeschool records for that year. That may be fun for the elementary grades, but for high school you will want to keep some of the work they did through the school year.

One of the colleges that we applied to asked for a math assignment in my student's handwriting. Yet another college asked for a science lab report. Yet another college asked for a graded

English paper. It can be difficult to know in advance what they're going to ask for. Keep a few samples of work from each class you teach and you'll be prepared for anything.

Final Review

The last step is the final review, which is like doing the dishes after Thanksgiving. Check for spelling and consistent fonts and formatting. Make sure you update the table of contents, and frequently back up your work.

You can save files on your computer, or email the document to a friend as an emergency backup. If you have an online email service like Gmail and you email your comprehensive record to yourself, you can still access your Gmail account from a different computer and have access to your comprehensive record should your computer crash. You can also use Carbonite or other online services for backup as well. Make sure that you work on your comprehensive record every year and that you back it up every year so that you don't lose it.

Remember, colleges will look at certain pieces of information to find out if a child is "Real, Ready, and Right". They will look at the transcript, read the entire application, and all those application essays. Those test scores will be checked over to make sure that they match what's on the transcript. They carefully read the letters of recommendation. Your homeschool records and course descriptions will also be looked over so that they can see if your child has taken all the necessary classes and are ready for college classes.

When you put these parts together with a nice cover and table of contents, you are creating a formidable document that screams "This Student is Well-Educated!" The comprehensive records we put together for our two sons received feedback from one college admission director that they were the "best documented transcripts and records" he had seen; that included from any student, public school, private school or homeschool! He told us that our records were the primary reason our boys were invited, along with 108 other top applicants that year to compete for 10 full-tuition scholarships offered by that university.

Now, granted, our comprehensive records didn't WIN two of those ten scholarships...my boys did that themselves. But the comprehensive records opened those formidable university doors so they could then walk on through!

Chapter 4

Don't Play Fair

That's not to say that all the colleges we approached were happy about our comprehensive records. Sadly, some colleges may resist a comprehensive record. They might deny it publicly, but there are some admissions officials who've grown quite comfortable with the cookie cutter kids they see coming through their doors. If all they have to deal with are a few numbers (e.g., GPA and SAT/ACT scores) and a few variables (e.g., the essay and the application) it makes the winnowing process easier. It protects their "intellectual capital," that is, how hard they have to think.

The college application is a great example of how colleges will use a standard form to quickly identify differentiators between students. Some colleges even go a step further and have a "common application" which removes more variability by sharing the same information between many colleges. This is great for students trying to balance their senior year academics with multiple college applications, but it doesn't make your job of distinguishing your student from the thousands of others any easier.

Most parents and students will dutifully play this game with the colleges. They only submit what is asked and they never question the rules.

We didn't do it that way.

An illustration will be helpful at this point. My husband works in recruiting and developing engineering talent at a large northwest aerospace concern (who will remain nameless, but happens to rhyme with "Rowing.") For a typical job opening there may be hundreds of applicants. As a hiring manager, all you see from these applicants is a 10,000 character resume that has all the formatting stripped away. Smart applicants use every one of those characters. Smarter applicants have learned to exchange some of those precious 10,000 characters into a brief cover letter that will discuss their unique qualifications and why they fit the specific job.

These people have found a way to use the system to give them an advantage. My husband reports that people who follow this strategy are more likely to be selected for an interview.

In our family, we followed a similar strategy. We knew our bank account wouldn't support the expense of a university education for both of our students at the same time. We knew our boys could get the necessary loans but we had moral and spiritual reasons to not want our kids saddled with debt when they got out of school.

We knew if we played by the rules, the chances of our children being "lost in the crowd" would be high. So we decided NOT to play by the rules. We didn't "cheat" per se, because there really aren't any documented rules. We just adopted a "liberal interpretation of the application process."

We Decided to Give More

I mean, no one said "we forbid you from giving us more information than what is in the application package." They didn't say anything at all. My guess is they never HAD to say anything about it before. Parents and students simply don't challenge the conventional wisdom about the way the game should be played.

We decided that sending in a comprehensive record was worth the risk of being rejected. We didn't want to force something on the colleges that they were dead set against. So, during our discussions with them, prior to applying, we would produce a course description from one of our kid's classes and casually ask, "So, would you be interested in getting this type of record from my students as part of their application package?"

The reactions from the colleges were very positive, but one admissions official said something that was at the same time both fascinating and revealing. After reading the course description very carefully, she smiled broadly and said "Not only do we want this, but I wish every student we reviewed was required to give this documentation." This same official confessed, "We see kids every day who have As and Bs on their high school transcript but when they get here, we discover they can't read or write, at least not at a high school level. You wouldn't believe how many of our new students need remedial classes before they are ready for college level work. Your comprehensive record gives us confidence that your students are well educated."

That was enough to convince us that time spent designing and creating our comprehensive record was worth the effort.

The Results Were AMAZING!

The results of including a comprehensive record in the admission package reinforced this decision. Three of the four colleges quickly admitted our children and the college scholarship offers started to pour in. Interestingly, there was one "fussy" college – one that is considered a "public ivy" - who initially said they didn't want the records. We were polite and sent them just what they asked for - a transcript and application. But we also snuck in the comprehensive record, "just in case."

The colleges who read our comprehensive record seemed to try to one-up each other with the most attractive financial packages. Our problem college, however, actually rejected our boys because they said we hadn't fulfilled their "special" requirements for homeschoolers. At that point, we knew the offers from the other schools were more than good enough.

There was a strong temptation to just blow off this fourth college but, frankly, I was a little miffed at them for being so unfriendly to homeschoolers.

I responded politely but firmly that we would not jump through their hoops and no additional subject tests would be coming. I told them to evaluate our students on the basis of their records. I told them to read their copy of our comprehensive record. We didn't hear from them for a couple of weeks and then we got the "fat letter" from their school saying our boys were admitted. Shortly thereafter they started sending us big, juicy scholarships as well!

What made the difference? Our boys hadn't changed and certainly their education hadn't changed. The ONLY thing that shifted was this university's perception of our students. It was the comprehensive record that forced this shift.

Ultimately, our comprehensive records helped us land scholarships totaling over $440,000 from the four schools where my boys applied, including $187,000 worth of full-tuition scholarships both my boys earned from their first choice university!!!

Chapter 5

"Do I REALLY Need a Comprehensive Record?"

It is true, you may not NEED a comprehensive record. In fact, I can think of four valid reasons why a comprehensive record might not be required for you.

- Your child isn't going to college.
- You have your heart set on only one college and they have told you in no uncertain terms NOT to send it to them.
- You've got a spare $200,000 lying around the house.
- Your student has perfect grades, perfect SAT scores, and enough

national recognition on their transcript to impress a PhD.

If this doesn't describe your child, then you would be well served to follow the Boy Scout Motto...

Always Be Prepared!

As a parent homeschooling high school, you wear a lot of hats, including teacher, principal, and school nurse. Mom may take the lead on teaching and nursing. Dad may step up to being the principal. But what about the other responsibilities?

- Who is going to be the guidance counselor?
- Who is going to "project manage" the college application process?
- Who will document your homeschool records?
- Who will make sure those records will completely and accurately represent your student and present them in the best possible light?

The answer is, of course, you — GULP!!

I will be honest with you. Putting together our comprehensive record was hard... REALLY Hard. It started with the fact that even though I am an organized person, I really didn't know the type of information I would need to build my student's records.

To top that off, when my youngest son was 15 years old, I "discovered" I needed to graduate him from high school the following year. Perhaps you can begin to sense the panic I was starting to feel about putting our records together.

Putting our comprehensive record together was sort of like our homeschool "Hail Mary" play at getting scholarships that would enable my kids to attend college without incurring massive debt. Can you feel my panic growing?!

My biggest concern was that there was absolutely NO TEMPLATE out there that could tell me what a comprehensive record ought to look like. We were breaking new ground. This fact was reinforced by the colleges who received our records who told me they had "never seen anything like it before." The quote from Bryan Jones from Seattle Pacific University is one of our favorites and we have it posted all over our website:

"Your homeschool transcripts and records were the best organized and documented I have seen."

There are many advantages to putting together a comprehensive record for your child - and really no downside. I strongly encourage you to get started today on yours - one step at a time.

Chapter 6

The Homeschool Olympics

I love watching the Olympic Games, but it seems like every four years the networks find at least one "tragic" story to share with the audience. Perhaps it's the Olympic skier who trains for 10 years only to fall 5 seconds out of the gate, or the marathon runner who gets incorrect information from the trainer and misses his qualifying heat. I guess it is the mixture of "the thrill of victory and the agony of defeat" that makes this such compelling television.

Homeschooling high school has a lot in common with preparing for the Olympics. There is rigorous training, coaching, preparation, and loads of practice. Then, after four years of hard work comes your student's opportunity to shine. What will the colleges say when you present your student to them?

Will they give them the Gold Medal, or will they be disqualified?

Just like the Olympics, the stakes are high. You play a critical role in preparing your "athlete". A beautiful comprehensive record is one great way for your family to "go for the gold."

Standing on the Podium

For me, one of the best feelings in the world was knowing that my husband and I did the very best job possible preparing our children for adult life: academically, socially and spiritually.

It is even sweeter knowing that we did everything in our power to help them attend the college of their dreams and then begin their adult life without the burden of crushing college debt.

We invested A LOT in our children's homeschool career. We struggled with insecurity and not knowing how we would pay for college. We trusted God...and worked like crazy! But of all the work, worry, and struggle, our success boiled down to this one indisputable fact: creating excellent comprehensive records for our boys had by far the BEST RETURN of any single investment we made as homeschool parents.

I believe you owe it to yourself and your family to embrace this challenge and develop a stunning homeschool comprehensive record that will AMAZE the colleges. You will be overwhelmed by the sweet feelings of pride and confidence you will gain by doing it.

Step Into My Time Machine

Before we go, I would like you to imagine the following scene just a few years into the future:

The college admission officer stares at the tsunami of application packages piled high on his desk. Diving in, he quickly and deftly dispatches package after package with fatal finality. "Boring," "cookie-cutter," "unprepared," are his unspoken judgments as the reject stack grows dangerously high. Now he's in the zone....

One package, however, stops him short. Leaning back in his chair he notes that this student has had a remarkable education, filled with challenging courses. They've had tremendous experiences not just in the world of students but also in the world of adults. They come across as well-rounded, mature, with a strong sense of self. "I Am a Leader!" seems to scream from every page.

The official instantly makes the admission decision. Noting that this is a homeschool student, he places that application apart from the unwashed bulk of rejects to be given special attention for the biggest scholarships his university has to offer.

The message is clear: **You want that to be your child!**

Now is the time to decide if you will make the effort to prepare your homeschool records in a way that will capture the attention of the colleges. I am here to help you!

I know you can do this!

Chapter 7

Helpful Resources

I hope this book has encouraged you to tackle comprehensive homeschool records for your own child. If you decide that you want more help to create such records, I have a couple of resources that can help you.

Do it Yourself Option:

If you would like to see the complete homeschool records we submitted for our oldest son, Kevin, as well as detailed information on how to prepare similar records yourself, you can purchase our book, "Setting the Records Straight: How to Craft Homeschool Transcripts and Course Descriptions for College Admission and Scholarships." Many parents have used this book as a template for creating their own records from scratch.

Training, Tools and Templates Option:

If you want more help and don't want to "reinvent the wheel", here is a link where you can get my Comprehensive Record Solution.

www.ComprehensiveRecordSolution.com

This resource will give you complete training on how we made our scholarship-winning comprehensive homeschool records, including all the templates, instructions and pre-made course descriptions you will need to quickly and painlessly complete this task. Take advantage of our experience and don't do this alone. You will be so glad you did! If you decide to order, and then send me an email (Lee@TheHomeScholar.com) letting me know you ordered through this Kindle book offer, **I will throw in my best selling Total Transcript Solution (a $47 value) for free.**

Afterword

Stories of Success

Creating beautiful homeschool records is serious work that can take a significant time commitment on the part of one or both parents. It is normal to ask "is it really worth it?" I wanted to share a few of the many success stories I have heard from homeschool parents just like you who tackled this task and succeeded beyond their wildest dreams.

"Hi Lee!!! Haven't contacted you since my senior, Bryan, was accepted into the University of North Carolina School of the Arts in April! I understand that they interviewed him with his "Comprehensive High School Record" open in their possession, referring to details within it during the interview! Wow — what fun to know that all that work was of value to them in their job of selecting candidates for their program. Thank you, Lee, for the unspeakably big help you were in that whole process of my documenting his high school years! I had done NO course descriptions until I started fall of last year!! Nightmare! — but your help and guidance got me through it beautifully (although exhausted) in time to submit it all in December! Well — my rising 10th and 11th graders are NOT going to be in the same place by the time THEIR applications are rolling — this mom's got some SERIOUS templates to work from, and multitudes of know-how, thanks to my personal HomeScholar tutor!"

~ Mary, homeschool mom to Bryan

"Lee's input enabled me to prepare a "Comprehensive High School Record" for my son which allowed me to present in a college-friendly format his uniqueness and his strengths, along with the details of the rigorous education he had received here at home. He was accepted into the college of his choice, and I received feedback from the academic dean and the admitting office that the content was exactly what they wanted to see for review purposes. I would not have known where to start without the specific and very encouraging help she gave."

~Mary, North Carolina

"It really made for a more professional look. You are providing a service much needed by many. Her scholarship will be paying for four years of tuition, out-of-state fees, room/board, book stipend as well as $5000 toward a month summer abroad program. Thank you again for all that I learned through your services."

~ Renee in Europe

"I wanted to present Nate's accomplishments in the best possible light, and I believe the course descriptions and small portfolio of work does a wonderful job of capturing what he accomplished in home school. I would NEVER have gotten this far without you... I probably would have given up or done something simple and not adequately reflective of Nate's high school. So the application materials are in the mail on their way to University!"

~Ann in Connecticut

"In applying for the summer institutes I used your model to the best of my ability. I watched the DVDs enough to have them pretty much set to memory. I plan on putting together a complete comprehensive record ASAP. I want to have available my son's accomplishments in a neat and presentable package. Without you, our homeschool would not be as organized record keeping and academically, and my younger kids' "specializations" may not be looked upon as blessings."

~Janel in North Dakota

"Real live samples, like the sample Course Description and Grades and Credits Resource sheet, really clarify things and give homeschoolers a starting point in creating their own, which is very helpful! The "Record Keeping" section was very good too. This topic and the way you present it would be extremely useful for parents new to homeschooling high school. I was impressed by your knowledge and insights. Basically, everything was excellent, and the bonuses added that extra special touch! God bless you!"

~Donna in Oregon

"Just wanted to shoot you a note to say THANK YOU. My daughter applied online to her first choice university. She had to send in a hard copy of her transcript. We sent that in, but in addition and thanks to your guidance, we also sent in a cover letter followed by her comprehensive record. Your assistance via the phone was invaluable and was a great confidence booster as we embarked on this journey."

~Chrystal in Georgia

To order my Comprehensive Record Solution, go to:

www.ComprehensiveRecordSolution.com

After you order, make sure to send me an email (Lee@TheHomeScholar.com) and I will add my Total Transcript Solution to your account for free ($47 value)

Appendix 1

Super-Size Scholarships with Outside Documentation

Public education is floundering and colleges are struggling to fill spots with qualified students, capable of working at a college level. Outside documentation can prove your child is worthy of college admission and scholarships! You see, colleges need to separate high school students who appear to be educated, from those who actually are well educated. High schools will often weight grades, so all their students will appear to be above average. To solve this problem, colleges look at outside documentation. To simplify things, colleges first look to subject tests that provide some proof that an applicant understands the classes listed on their high school transcript. But honestly, tests aren't enough.

Outside documentation is more than a test score. There are a variety of sources that colleges use to determine college readiness. Whether a child is a good test-taker or not, there is a source for outside documentation that will be a perfect fit. Spend some time and think about how you can provide outside documentation for your homeschool. You can give colleges the information they need in a variety of different ways and increase your child's chances of college admission and scholarships!

SAT Subject Tests

The most common outside documentation provided by public, private, and homeschool students are subject tests. SAT Subject Tests (or SAT II Tests) are available by subject and are a proven way to provide outside documentation. These are high school level tests. Each test is one hour long and the questions are mostly multiple-choice. Subjects include French, U.S. History, Chemistry, Math, and many others. Some colleges require these tests of all applicants. A few may require more subject tests from homeschoolers than the general public. Some colleges ask for five, others ask for only three, while many don't require any. Find out testing requirements while searching for the right college in order to ensure your child qualifies for admission. These subject tests are a great option for most students who test well.

AP Tests

Advanced Placement (AP) Tests can also demonstrate your child's mastery of a subject. Sometimes AP tests are required by colleges. AP tests are college level tests, allowing your child to earn college credit with good scores, depending on each college's policy. There are over 30 different subjects available to choose from. Each test includes short and long essay questions along with multiple choice questions.

Homeschoolers take these tests at their local public or private high school. While AP courses are available, your child is not required to complete an AP course; they can simply take the test. Because AP classes are so rigorous and time-consuming, make sure to keep an eye on the big picture. A well-rounded, happy, educated student will look more appealing to colleges than a child who has passed a slew of AP exams with nothing else to show for it.

If your child gets burned out by large numbers of difficult classes, or doesn't have time to complete core subjects like math or science, then AP courses may actually hurt them in the long run.

Many colleges will provide college credit for passing AP scores, which can reduce college costs. These tests are the best choice for children applying to Ivy League or highly selective colleges. They are an excellent choice for students who test well, write well, and are academically capable and hard-working.

CLEP Exams

CLEP exams (College Level Examination Program) are great tests for providing outside documentation at the college level. CLEP exams are designed for non-traditional learners, and are available year-round at local testing centers and community colleges.

There are over 30 different subjects to choose from, with no age limits placed on the exams. They are often used by adult learners returning to college and less often by high school students, who may typically take AP exams instead. Upon completion of each exam, an official transcript is sent to your chosen colleges.

CLEP exams prove to colleges that your child is capable of college level work. Some colleges will provide college credit for passing a CLEP exam, which can dramatically reduce college costs and shorten the time to earn a degree. Other colleges will use the exams to place your student in higher level classes, which will serve to keep them challenged and may also reduce overall costs.

These tests are great option for students that learn naturally at a high level, read a lot, and test well on a computer. They are an excellent option for students applying to a college that will provide college credit for each passing exam.

Dual Enrollment

Some high school students take classes at their community college. Students receive high school credit and college credit at the same time, which is why it is called dual enrollment. Taking courses at the community college can prove that your child is capable of college level work.

Community college can be a "Rated R" environment, requiring maturity and confidence. If you choose this option, I suggest you use the "buddy system" and have your children take each class with other homeschoolers. Take care choosing each class professor by looking at RateMyProfessor.com. Look over the textbook and required reading prior to the first day of class to ensure there are no unpleasant surprises.

For outside documentation, it's best to take a community college class in each different core subject area. In other words, try to get at least one class in English, Math, Science, Foreign Language, Social Science, and Fine Art. Explain to your children the importance of getting excellent grades, preferably all As, in all community college classes, so they are the most appealing to admissions officers.

Community college classes can shorten the college path, and therefore save a lot of money on the cost of a college degree. If you are applying to a university, be careful not to take community college classes after high school graduation, because that can eliminate some scholarship opportunities. This is often not a good option for Christian families who would not consider a non-Christian university because of the environment. This can be a great option for mature, smart kids who may not test well but are willing to work hard academically.

Letters of Recommendation

A letter of recommendation describes the qualities, characteristics, and capabilities of the student, explaining how they will function at college and bring positive attributes to the college campus. The best letter of recommendation will be written by an adult who knows your child well and can write well. They should be eager and willing to write a glowing recommendation.

Community college professors are a great source. Make sure your child gets to know their professors. Encourage them to sit in the front row, ask questions, participate, and visit their professors during office hours. A glowing recommendation is more likely from a college professor who knows the student by name, and can comment on their work ethic.

If your child doesn't take community college classes, they can obtain letters of recommendation from other sources, such as apprenticeships, internships, and job experiences. The student requests a letter of recommendation from an adult they know. When the person agrees, your child can give them a copy of their transcript, activity list, or resume, so they have a fuller view of the student's abilities. A letter of recommendation is often required during the college admission process. This is an excellent option for students who develop close relationships with professors or adults in leadership positions.

Comprehensive Records

As we've discussed, comprehensive homeschool records go beyond a simple transcript, and include course descriptions, reading list, activity list, and work samples for college admission. These records provide extra-special documentation of thorough academic preparation, and they can be a key to obtaining college admission and scholarships.

Some colleges are happy to know you have this information, and when they see a large package of information will gleefully think "Woo Hoo! We have one of those awesome homeschool parents who goes over-the-top academically!" Other schools will read and savor every word you write, thankful for this additional information they may require from homeschoolers. Some colleges will deny they want these records, until they need them. Those are the schools that might question just one class, and in lieu of outside documentation through tests, might be willing to read your thorough documentation from your course description to fill that gap.

This is an excellent option for parents who push their children academically or include delight-directed learning, but do not have a lot of outside classes. I recommend creating transcripts and course descriptions for every homeschool child, but they are absolutely critical for parents who don't have other outside documentation, or need scholarships in order to afford college, or are applying to elite colleges.

Work Résumé

How do adults provide outside documentation? By providing a résumé! A work résumé is a short document describing education, work history, references, and a list of achievements given to an employer when applying for a job. This same style of information can be presented to colleges, to demonstrate extraordinary work experience.

What are colleges looking for, anyway? They are looking for committed young people who are willing to work hard for the goals they want to achieve. What could demonstrate hard work more than a list of ways the student has already worked hard? A strong résumé, along with a high school transcript and diploma, will be required by employers, if the child does not go to college. This is a wonderful option for students that have a lot of work experience instead of a lot of academic experience.

Performance or Competition

Instead of tests, some colleges will ask for performance from the student when they visit the campus. This may be a formal interview experience, or an informal event with a student or graduate from the college. If your child will be interviewed, make sure you prepare them for the experience. Often these interviews can determine whether the student is admitted or not, and how much scholarship money will be awarded. If you are preparing your child for a campus interview, read "How to Win a Scholarship Competition and Ace the Admission Interview" on my website, www.TheHomeScholar.com.

For fine art students, their art portfolio provides outside documentation that can be as important as academics - or even more important. Music students will often be asked to audition with their instrument, even multiple times, competing against other artists for limited spots. Fine art applications are unique, so you want to carefully do your research and thoroughly research each college for their application requirements. I suggest that fine art students attend a Performing and Visual Arts College Fair. This is a great option for children with a special gift or talent, and will likely be required by fine art conservatories and fine art university programs.

Application Essays

College application essays explain in writing the character qualities of the student. Each college may request the student write one to four written papers, and they may be short (250 words) or long (1,000 words). These are self-reflective personal essays that answer the question "Who are you?"

These essays must be technically perfect descriptive essays that demonstrate the strength of the student's writing ability. These essays explain exactly why the student is ready for college, and why they are a good fit for each particular school. So really, a college admission essay is a "selfie" in words, carefully showing exactly who the student is, from multiple perspectives. Don't repeat anything between essays, and certainly don't repeat anything on the essay that is already on your application or transcript. This is no time to be wasting words on a list of accomplishments or classes or test scores that the college should already know from the rest of your application. A poor writer can take as much time as they need during the writing process to create a great written "selfie." This is an excellent option for all children applying to colleges, and I recommend it for everyone.

Colleges value homemade homeschool records, but sometimes they want to see more. Sometimes colleges want to see outside documentation, such as standardized tests or community college classes to demonstrate a student's abilities. Usually a transcript along with college admission test scores is sufficient for college applications, but additional documentation can be helpful when searching for scholarships or gaining admission to elite universities. Outside documentation can help prove that your child has the knowledge necessary to succeed in college.

There are many ways to provide outside documentation to colleges. Consider each one carefully and choose the ones that will help your child earn college admission and scholarships. You know your child, so trust your judgment! Find the perfect fit for your family.

Appendix 2

What Do You Really Need to Keep?

A military mom shares her frustrations with homeschool record keeping.

"How much of my kids' elementary or middle school paper work do I need to keep? I have every notebook, every workbook they have done. We just moved for the third summer in a row and as I moved that stuff, one more time, it got me thinking do I really need to keep all of it? I have tests and grades in a separate binder, but do I need to keep all their workbooks?"

~ Melissa, Military Mom

The volume of records you keep depends on what you want to do with the information. There are three purposes for homeschool records you will want to keep in mind.

1. Obey state law

I always encourage people to obey their state homeschool laws; you might be asked to keep certain information while you are homeschooling. I haven't heard of any state that requires tons of information, though. Check your state law to see. It's often just a report card and some test scores. Beyond that, most records can be kept on your computer. Here's a tip: think about what a public school keeps from one year to the next. They don't keep EVERY piece of paper, just a report card and test scores. Regardless of where you move, states can only demand you meet their requirements during the time you live there, so you still don't have to keep everything forever.

2. Apply to college

When keeping records for college application, the situation changes a bit. Keep enough information to describe your class in a course description and make a transcript. That means keeping quite a bit of information, at least until you get those documents done. You also want to have some samples of work from each class – a written paper or math test, for example. Keep enough information to create a reading list and activity list, too. All this information means one thing – you don't have to keep anything from elementary school or even 7th and 8th grade level classes for the purposes of college admission.

3. Keep mementos

If you don't need something for state law, and you don't need it for college admission, then just do a quick "Do I love it?" check. If it's a memento you want to keep, then keep it because you LOVE it – not because it's homeschool work, but because it is a reminder of their childhood. It's like keeping their first baby outfit. It may not be important for "school" but it's still important to your family.

Let me give you an example. In elementary school I kept a running total of curriculum tests, and we didn't use many. I kept the annual assessments my kids took each year, and our state-required Declaration of Intent to Homeschool. In middle school, I kept more records as I tried to learn how to homeschool high school. By the time 9th grade came around, I was keeping one 3-ring notebook of material for each child for each year of school, which I condensed into comprehensive homeschool records and course descriptions for college admission.

If you feel you need more help with your homeschool records, check out my Comprehensive Record Solution for everything you need to help keep great records!

www.ComprehensiveRecordSolution.com

Afterword

Who is Lee Binz and What Can She Do for Me?

Number one best-selling homeschool author, Lee Binz is The HomeScholar. Her mission is "helping parents homeschool high school." Lee and her husband Matt homeschooled their two boys, Kevin and Alex, from elementary through high school.

Upon graduation, both boys received four-year, full tuition scholarships from their first choice university. This enables Lee to pursue her dream job - helping parents homeschool their children through high school.

On The HomeScholar website, you will find great products for creating homeschool transcripts and comprehensive records to help you amaze and impress colleges.

Find out why Andrew Pudewa, Director of the Institute for Excellence in Writing says, "Lee Binz knows how to navigate this often confusing and frustrating labyrinth better than anyone."

You can find Lee online at:

www.TheHomeScholar.com

If this book has been helpful, could you please take a minute to write us a quick review on Amazon?

Thank you!

Testimonials

The Best Resource on Homeschooling High School

"WOW!!!!!! I love the Comprehensive Record Solution. This resource contains it all!! This product is going to save many homeschool parents time, energy and money. It is by far the best resource I have seen on homeschooling high school for college preparation and admission. The written information is clear, concise and easy to use. The audio/video portions are easy to listen to and your chatty conversation-like style puts the overwhelmed homeschooler at ease. And you speak in the videos like a girlfriend who is going through all the same stuff with me! I feel myself saying, "YES!!! That was your experience too?!" It is soooo affirming. Your product is worth every penny and I can't wait to recommend this new resource to all of my homeschooling friends. Great job and thank you so much for sharing your work, energy, time and expertise with the rest of us. You have been the best resource for my homeschool high school."

~ Sally in Washington

Very Professional and Detailed

"Sooo, I asked for feedback on my son's high school transcripts I submitted for early college. Since this is my first time homeschooling all the way through, I was pleased with these words: "You did an incredible job in putting everything together; the transcript, the course descriptions, the book list and report card. It is very professional and detailed. Typically more information is better than less. When I saw the records I thought it was a private school."

~ Valerie

For more information about my **Total Transcript Solution** and **Comprehensive Record Solution**, go to:

www.TotalTranscriptSolution.com and www.ComprehensiveRecordSolution.com

Also From The HomeScholar...

- The HomeScholar Guide to College Admission and Scholarships: Homeschool Secrets to Getting Ready, Getting In and Getting Paid (Book and Kindle Book)
- Setting the Records Straight - How to Craft Homeschool Transcripts and Course Descriptions for College Admission and Scholarships (Book and Kindle Book)
- Preparing to Homeschool High School (DVD)
- Finding a College (DVD)
- The Easy Truth About Homeschool Transcripts (Kindle Book)

- Parent Training A la Carte (Online Training)
- Total Transcript Solution (Online Training, Tools and Templates)
- Comprehensive Record Solution (Online Training, Tools and Templates)
- Gold Care Club (Comprehensive Online Support and Training)
- Homeschool "Convention at Home" Kit (Book, DVDs and Audios)

The HomeScholar "Coffee Break Books" Released or Coming Soon on Kindle and Paperback:

- Delight Directed Learning: Guiding Your Homeschooler Toward Passionate Learning
- Creating Transcripts for Your Unique Child: Help Your Homeschool Graduate Stand Out from the Crowd
- Beyond Academics: Preparation for College and for Life
- Planning High School Courses: Charting the Course Toward High School Graduation
- Graduate Your Homeschooler in Style: Make Your Homeschool Graduation Memorable

- Keys to High School Success: Get Your Homeschool High School Started Right!
- Getting the Most Out of Your Homeschool This Summer: Learning just for the Fun of it!
- Finding a College: A Homeschooler's Guide to Finding a Perfect Fit
- College Scholarships for High School Credit: Learn and Earn With This Two-for-One Strategy!
- College Admission Policies Demystified: Understanding Homeschool Requirements for Getting In
- A Higher Calling: Homeschooling High School for Harried Husbands (by Matt Binz, Mr. HomeScholar)
- Gifted Education Strategies for Every Child: Homeschool Secrets for Success
- College Application Essays: A Primer for Parents
- Creating Homeschool Balance: Find Harmony Between Type A and Type Zzz...
- Homeschooling the Holidays: Sanity Saving Strategies and Gift Giving Ideas
- Your Goals this Year: A Year by Year Guide to Homeschooling High School

- Making the Grades: A Grouch-Free Guide to Homeschool Grading
- High School Testing: Knowledge That Saves Money
- Getting the BIG Scholarships: Learn Expert Secrets for Winning College Cash!
- Easy English for Simple Homeschooling: How to Teach, Assess and Document High School English
- Scheduling - The Secret to Homeschool Sanity: Plan You Way Back to Mental Health
- Junior Year is the Key to High School Success: How to Unlock the Gate to Graduation and Beyond
- Upper Echelon Education: How to Gain Admission to Elite Universities
- How to Homeschool College: Save Time, Reduce Stress and Eliminate Debt
- Homeschool Curriculum That's Effective and Fun: Avoid the Crummy Curriculum Hall of Shame!
- Comprehensive Homeschool Records: Put Your Best Foot Forward to Win College Admission and Scholarships
- Options After High School: Steps to Success for College or Career

- How to Homeschool 9th and 10th Grade: Simple Steps for Starting Strong!
- Senior Year Step-by-Step: Simple Instructions for Busy Homeschool Parents
- High School Math The Easy Way: Simple Strategies for Homeschool Parents In Over Their Heads

Would you like to be notified when we offer the next *Coffee Break Books* for FREE during our Kindle promotion days? If so, leave your name and email below and we will send you a reminder.

http://www.TheHomeScholar.com/freekindlebook.php

Visit my Amazon Author Page!

amazon.com/author/leebinz

64712054R00060

Made in the USA
Lexington, KY
17 June 2017